THE DEPTHS OF HIS LOVE

MY MEMOIR

BEATRICE BELINDA

I dedicate this book to my daughters, Shyla and Mariela. They are the ones who light the room when they walk in and warm my heart with their love. This book is for all the women who needed to heal the little girl inside of them. I hope my words can help lead you to the path of healing.

DISCLAIMER

This is a work of creative nonfiction. The events are portrayed to the best of Beatrice Belinda's memory. While all the stories in this book are true, some names and identifying details have been changed to protect people's privacy.

ACKNOWLEDGMENTS

Painful experiences can produce more heartache or allow you to be grateful for what you have. I decided on the latter. Because of my experiences, I can see the real meaning of love. I thank God for the strength through those moments. I am thankful to my parents for always believing in me and helping me through the most challenging moments in my life. I am grateful to my daughters for being my driving force to continue forward. I fight harder and strive for more because they motivate me to change the world by changing *my* world. My family and friends were always of aid in my moments of healing. Thank you.

PROLOGUE

Have you ever been here? Here, in this place of loneliness, where the echoes of your internal dialogue overwhelm you with the thought of ending your own life. I know I am not alone in this feeling. We, as humans, can relate to this; we crave to love and be loved. Your desire to be loved is valid, no matter the gender, size, age, or ethnicity. We are all reminded every day through the media or traditional norms that we must be loved. The lack of love will leave us lonely. Feeling incomplete, unworthy, and not enough. Loneliness is a desperate and vacant feeling left in one's heart.

When we are lonely, we are disoriented and can make decisions that will not benefit us in the long run. We sometimes want to fill the void with people, substances, and habits to help us cope with our lonely hearts. We often don't anticipate the adverse effects. We create destructive ways to avoid hurt or loneliness.

Genesis 2:18, KJV

And the LORD God said, it is not good that the man should be alone; I will make him help meet for him.

Loneliness can be the symptom of any illnesses that traces to the heart. In prisons, the punishment is often solitary confinement, and what a punishment it is. I truly believe we choose the partners we *think* we deserve. We choose them based on our foundation of what we believe love is and what we think we deserve. I want first to clarify I do not think women or men deserve to be in an abusive relationship. We all want to be loved and search for that subconsciously, guided by our internal dialogue. When I was a kid, my dream was to be loved and, more importantly, I wanted to get married to see that love. Being married seemed to be a direct correlation that defined love and how I wanted to be loved. That definition of love was founded on shaky ground.

I based my definition of love on the superficial representation of a soap opera, flaky family members, and distrusting friends. I found my passion for how others felt about me and the diminishing perspective of empty people. My internal dialogue fed me lies, and I was my enemy. I went to great lengths to experience that love. The repeated conversation within my soul established every type of love I tried to uncover with my relationships. When I hit rock bottom, the recurring thoughts were that I just wanted to be loved, noticed, cared for, worthy, to matter, to be understood, to escape, to be someone's world, to feel wanted, to feel safe, enough, to heal, and to be saved. My heart and soul were fueled with words that my friends, family, enemies, and societal norms had imprinted on me. Feeling like I did not have a voice, I had to find it. I could not allow the loneliness that plagued my soul to consume me because this was not living. That borrowed mindset had me existing in a world that put me in a box, that made their perspective conform to what they thought I should be like. This is my story of finding love in an unloving relationship.

1

TO BE LOVED

True love seems like a variety of definitions for the receiver. For the orphan, love is the one who stays. For the abused, it is the one who accepts me. It is the substitutionary sacrifice of my life for the Christ believer, my life for yours. We can define true love as avoid needing to be filled. In Psychology, it is believed to be a need to achieve self-actualization and achieve a sense of completion.

I wanted to be loved. It was my goal since I was a little girl. My definition of love stemmed from what the media told me love was. The prince always saves the princess, and, in my case, he was also the male lead in the soap opera. There was something beautiful about having someone on your side through conflict and turmoil.

As a child, I didn't *feel* loved. This sounds like such a selfish statement, I know. Let me explain. I always have had loving parents. We were all looked after, fed, clothed, and acknowledged. I didn't feel loved. I felt like a burden like I wasted time and space on this earth and was merely an extra. Not necessary, not enough, not worthy. I say this because this is important. This is the root of where I identified self-love. This is where my venture of a lifetime of habits of self-loathing began. I had to tell myself what I felt was valid, meaningful, and mattered. This statement is big for me. I did not express these feelings to anyone at the time.

I never spoke about anything to avoid burdening someone with my child-like mindset. The youngest of four, I felt overlooked and the unimportant child. The other three children exhausted my mother, so she spent her days after work with migraines and a list of errands to complete. My father was a pastor, always assisting the community's needs and helping the poor. In a picture-perfect world, I had nothing to complain about. I had a mother who took care of her children and a father who was a provider to his family and the community. But I always questioned why I was born this way. It was almost as if I was born with a broken heart, and I was looking for someone to fix it. These are my feelings and are my beginning, and I owned it. These were my feelings, and they are valid. This experience was my foundation of self-love. I thought if I experienced love in the way I fantasized, it would fix what was wrong.

If you are trying to have someone accept your perspective from your direct experience, remember that we don't see things with the same mindset. In psychology, this is called differential susceptibility. Two siblings can be parented the same way, but they will not have the same experience. Therefore, not everyone feels loved the same way.

NOVELA LOVE

It was a family tradition to gather around the TV set at 7:00 p.m. as we ate dinner. We all tuned into the Spanish channel Univision, and there was our favorite soap opera. We were watching *Mauricio's Love* and excited for the grand finale. We expected to learn more after the epic cliffhanger the Friday before.

"*Mauricio Como Puedes*?" Belinda asked as she read his note.

"*Si mi amor, perdoname!*" he pleaded.

"*Mauricio para ti, te doy mi vida.*"

A tear ran from my eye, and I quickly wiped it away. I glazed the room to see my mom and sisters clenching their blankets in anticipation.

"*Belinda, NO,*" Mauricio cried.

As Belinda was shot from behind, she said, "*Te Amo.*"

The blood filled his hands as he soon realized the villain was his mother all along.

As Mauricio gave Belinda his last kiss, she took her last breath for eternity.

"May our souls become one in heaven," he whispered in her ear as her body lay cold in his arms.

Betrayal, love, and passion all in one scene. What will Mauricio do with his dying love for Belinda?

-

Despair, sadness, and emptiness spread across the room as the Martinez women finished the finale of Mauricio's Love.

As the credits ended, I watched the blank screen, hopeful for a plot twist. May his love not to be in vain, I thought.

My moment of excitement quickly disappeared when my sister Susan threw the blanket in my face.

"It's your turn. *Stupida,*" Susan said.

"What? No. I did it last week," I quickly responded.

"No, but you missed like two days, and you put all the food down the drain, so that does not count." Susan was trying to find a way to avoid washing dishes.

"No, do not come at me with that. I am not doing jack," I answered, flustered.

"Mami, MIRA ESTA!" Susan hollered.

Before I could encounter the wrath of my mother, I ran into my room. I locked the door behind me and raced to my knees, then realized I scuffed my knees on the floor. I ran into my closet and grabbed my pink backpack as I leaned against the wall when a flicker of wallpaper fell on my eyelid and post-it notes from my wall of prayers. I found it. As a tear rolled down my cheek and onto the chain of the locket, I prayed.

"I want a love like this. I want a love that does not break or bend, a malleable love like Mauricio. An unconditional, sacrificial love."

As I opened the locket, the key fell out at that moment, and it felt as if it was glowing.

I continued to pray and said, "God, may the man who truly loves me have the key to my heart."

Interrupted from my fantasy *novela*, my mom knocked on the door. "Whose turn, is it?"

As she spoke, my mind faded into my one thought: One day, a man will have the key to my heart, and I prayed insistently for this loneliness to disappear.

My mother grew frustrated as I was not responding, and I threw a blanket over my head as I heard muffles of screams in the background. My vision blurred, my hands were sweaty, and my heart was racing. The thumps on my chest reverberated through my jacket. I put my headphones on to pretend I could not hear. I would turn on my flashlight and open my bible to the center where a *Novela* digest of *Mauricio's Love* was.

Looking back, I realized that, oh my goodness, the drama, the false depiction that love had to correlate with extreme and inconsistent behaviors. I held this image of love onto an extreme ideal of what a relationship should be.

John 3:16

   For God so loved the world that he gave his only begotten son.

Because of this verse, I wanted to be worth dying for. I wanted a man to bear the weight of my expectations of saving me from myself. In my mind, this was true love.

Note: We can always look back on our foundation of how we identified love. For many, it will be different, but we must acknowledge our past to heal. We must admit what hurts and what's challenging to say. Healing wounds requires work and honesty toward us to realize our beginning from our point of view. What you felt matters because you begin to practice self-love once you acknowledge yourself. To love another, you must love yourself. You can't fill another's cup when your cup is empty. *Please take five minutes, and I dare you to write out what love is for you!*

2

TO BE NOTICED

Defining love is not as simple as the face value we portray. It is a profound human experience. When you feel invisible, how can you ever acknowledge or notice someone loving you? When you think you are being loved, you feel like the person notices you and sees you for who you are. Growing up, my vulnerability to being bullied easily made me feel like I wasn't seen for who I was. I never understood why I was an easy target. They pointed my imperfections out, but my positive traits were invisible. Feeling invisible will always make me want to hide and wallow in my self-pity. I know I am not the only one to feel that way.

I wanted to be noticed like Moses by the water. "She saw that he was a special baby and kept him hidden for three months" (**Exodus 2:2**). The pharaoh's daughter was able to notice this child by the water. I wanted God to shine a light on me so the right person could save me from the streams of sadness I was swimming in. I noticed a sad pattern in my life that everywhere I would go, I was bullied for how my nose and body looked. I tried everything to hide my flaws, so they would only see the good things I had to offer...

SOMETHING WRONG WITH ME

Another morning passed, and I felt the sun's harshness through my covers. As I opened my eyes, my mom pulled the blankets from my face.

"*Mira, nena*, wake up. You have to go to school."

Underwhelmed by going to school, I shrugged my shoulders and tried to turn over again.

My mom took my blanket and threw it on the side of the bed.

"Beatrice, and do not think I forgot you are washing the dishes when you come back from school!" she hollered.

"No, ma, I do not want to," I responded with frustration.

"I am not asking you. Get up. You have five minutes!" she demanded.

I threw on my highlighter green jacket and wrinkled

shirt from the laundry I did not bother to clean last Friday. I put some water on my hair and left my curly hair unbrushed. I rolled up my dirty sleeves underneath my oversized coat.

"Beatrice! I am going to be late!" Mom screamed.

I put my mismatched socks and shoes on and raced to the minivan.

"I have to drop your sisters off too! I cannot sign you in. Let them know that I will call them with a late note."

"I hate..."

"What did you say?"

"Nothing, *MA*."

"Do good and get good grades. Now get out!"

As I walked in slowly at the school entrance, my mother honked the horn.

"Ma," I grunted.

"Hurry up. You are going to be late for the first period."

The Jessicas noticed the loud noise from behind the minivan.

"Beatrice, your minivan is as ugly as you."

I ran past the three Jessica's.

"God, I hate it here," I whispered.

"Hey lesbian, I was talking to you." Jessica A said.

I looked to the side to see the other Jessica's there.

Jessica B pulled out the slit inside my gym bag.

"Oh, look, the ugly duckling wants to be a swan."

"Leave me alone," I grunted.

"Excuse me, what?" Jessica C said.

"Leave me alone!" I screamed, running through the halls.

I ran to an abandoned stall in the gym locker room. I covered my mouth in fear of the Jessica's hearing me. As I tried to catch my breath, I quickly locked the door.

I grabbed my headphones and turned on my music to my favorite song, *Falling in Love with Jesus,* by Kirk Whalum. I tucked my feet in hopes of the Jessica's not seeing me.

I finally relaxed as I was in tune with the music. I saw the three of Jessica's matching Nike sneakers and heard them whispering to each other from underneath the stall.

I covered my mouth as my body jerked and shook. The sensation of impending doom had returned.

I hope I do not pee on myself this time. God, please make them go away, I thought.

They threw my slit on the stall bathroom floor after drenching it with dirty toilet water.

"Next time, we will get you lesbo-piggy," the Jessica's chanted in unison.

As I laid my head back in the stall bathroom, I clenched the locket and closed my eyes.

Being bullied became a large rock I would stumble on for the rest of my young adult life. I allowed the words others would say about me to be words of truth. Choosing our partners is not only a simple decision as to their attractiveness, but it is also based on our experiences. Also, because of the type of people we spent time with.

The ability to place boundaries on toxic people is critical in stopping the cycle of abuse in any relationship. But if we cannot hold ourselves in a light worthy of being admired, we won't stop that cycle. If you want to be noticed, you must first see the beauty within yourself. It isn't until we overcome our hurt that we can accept the love waiting for us.

We may want to be noticed, but sometimes we already are. It may not be by a romantic partner, but others often see the good we do. When other people cannot acknowledge and know why you deserve love, it does not mean that you are any less deserving. Joseph was a great man of God and was still overlooked. We know the story with his jealous brothers.

Genesis 37:3

Now Israel loved Joseph more than all his children because he was the son of his old age: and he made him a coat of many colors.

Joseph was noticed and stood out, but others may not see it as positive. So much so that his brothers felt the need to sell him. We want to be loved by those who don't know how to love themselves. They cannot give us what they don't have.

Note: Sometimes, life can feel defined by our narrow perspective. We can identify ourselves from our upbringing and stand out negatively. But in all reality, those differences are just more reasons to love yourself. A lot of our self-hate originates from the negative self-talk we engage in. It is hard to see that you are being noticed. God gave me what I was asking for, to shine like a bright light. And I did, but the light was glaring the eyes of those with a heavy heart. I wanted my pain to be noticed because I was suffering in silence. *Please take five minutes, and I dare you to write what makes you feel noticed!*

3

TO BE CARED FOR

I was wanting to be noticed and seen as a vital part of feeling loved. I saw it go hand in hand with being cared for. As I went through life and the experiences that hardship and pain produced. I learned more about myself. No tear was ever in vain. I realized I wanted to be cared for and looked at with a warm, reassuring eye. I liked the comfort of knowing someone would stand up for me when I was put down and vulnerable. Remember when the soap opera series lead had protected their damsel in moments of distress?

I wanted someone to grab me from the depths of my pain and vulnerability and wrap me in their arms like a bird with a broken wing. I wanted my loved ones to see what was going on inside my heart. I felt helpless. I tried to communicate, but I could not find the words to express my genuine feelings. The basis of love starts with our family, or the lack thereof. We choose our partners to fill the void we think they can supply. In my experience, I wanted a prince to save me from the dark tower of loneliness I locked myself in. The key to leaving that tower is the freedom of the pain that stemmed from those feelings. Never invalidate your emotions and your reasons you want to feel loved. Learning more about those reasons can free you from expecting love from others and heal you from the wounds that keep you from freedom.

When David was picked last of all his brothers, he must have felt insufficient. The prophet Solomon asked David's father about his sons, and David wasn't mentioned. That must have made him feel small. I believe where we stand in our family has a lot to do with identifying love. He asked him where the future King is, and the Father did not even consider David as a candidate. This reminds me of a time growing up...

GROWING UP

Rhode Island, 2001, I started the fourth grade. I remember being sad much of the time. I compared myself and my appearance with my classmates. I thought I had to fulfill this quota to be accepted. The whole fourth grade was a blur. I was more in my head. When I sat at the kitchen table on a Friday night from my busy school week, I remember being excited to start the weekend. My father had just ordered pizza, and I was hungry! I sat down and ate two slices of pizza with the family. I then went upstairs and watched TV for thirty minutes before going back down to grab another slice of pizza. This time, my grandma was eyeing me. She yelled at me, saying if I continued that way, I would die of diabetes. With my family surrounding the table, I felt helpless and ashamed. I expected someone to defend me because I did not think

I was doing anything wrong. When no one did, I ran upstairs in tears.

Another time, my mind was cluttered with negative thoughts that overwhelmed me. I was at a parent-teacher conference, and my mom called my name. She told me, "Mi Amor, I am afraid you are going to stay back," as she read Mrs. Read's progress report.

Immediately, I thought, *oh great, my feelings are confirmed. I am a loser—something else for someone to make fun of me. I hate myself more than ever.*

My mom saw my eyes and told me, "I promise mi Amor, I will make it up to you." At that moment, I think Mami realized I wanted to be noticed. But unfortunately, these weren't the best circumstances. I felt better because Mrs. Read wasn't picking on me. She did it because she cared about me and was genuinely concerned. She made me read fifty books that summer. She gave me a list, and my mom brought me to the library. I felt noticed. I felt loved.

Despite the circumstance, Mrs. Read gave me hope. She let me know trying again is a second chance to become better, and you are not a loser because of it. That summer, I had stacked the books to my side and read them one by one. My child-like vanity mirror as a desk and a wooden four-by-four elevate me. I was in love with reading. Mrs. Read knew that would make me feel better. I returned to my second chance in fourth grade, and I nailed it. I was a rock star. Similar experiences can reflect how complicated the family dynamics can be and how we have critical moments when feeling loved by our family makes a significant impact!

In most cases, family is not blood but those willing to bleed for you. The type of natural love that creates a bond with your family is vital. That type of love is reflected in the story of Lazarus and how Mary and Martha went to great lengths to save their brother. Or Noah when his wife and children showed unity by joining him on the ark. The type of love for your family is naturally embedded, but not everyone will experience it. We cannot deny its influence on how we select our partner.

Note: We can have a village surrounding us and not know how we feel. We may hold them responsible for not protecting us in our vulnerability. But in our experiences, we can help others with an empathetic heart. We can reach a deeper level of love in vulnerability. We grow stronger by the thorns that prick our hands than the petals that fall from the stem. *Please take five minutes, and I dare you to describe how it feels like to be cared for!*

4

TO BE WORTHY

The love and support of your family can be fantastic if you are fortunate enough to have it, but the ability to love yourself is the foundation of your love. I want to tell you my love story, but it starts before meeting a man or falling in love; it began with my definition of being worthy. I was my worst enemy. I wanted to be worthy. How I loved myself prepared me for allowing others to love me and the boundaries I set for myself. My first glimpse of discovering true love was when I attempted to take my own life, to remove the pain stamped on my chest. My ability to believe that I was inadequate led me to create a pattern of behavior that was like a form of toxic escapism. I experienced something that would define my self-love in my late teenage years.

THE ATTEMPT

I was asked to preach in a church I was unfamiliar with, but the invite was as ambiguous as the week I was having. I struggled to search deep within to find the right words to offer God's people. I had an overwhelming deep pain in my chest. I felt undeserving of the gracious invitation to preach at the church. When I took a shower, I was deep in thought. I was flooded with negative thoughts in a pool of clean water. The opportunity was something I dreamt of. I felt inadequate, and I internally reasoned that being alive was the actual burden. The tears rolled down my face as I whispered, "I am a fraud. I am not worthy. Why can't I feel loved?"

I grabbed my throat with a tight grip and tried to drown myself in my greatest fear. To be alone, to die with a heart so lonely that no one would even notice I was gone. I felt faint and heard a soft voice speak to me. *I love you, and you are enough. You are not a mistake.* Hearing those words vibrating in my soul, I gasped for air and returned to color. Breathing heavily, I sobbed. I did not understand why, but I felt I was not worthy of doing something so special. They must've gotten confused about who they invited, and I felt like a complete imposter.

My inability to behave lovingly to myself and acknowledge my truth came to the surface with patterns of behavior that didn't serve me well. A part of me questioned why I always reverted mentally to seeking an escape. Why, when doing something good, did I believe that leaving this earth would finally prove what I wanted to know all along?

The sermon I was preparing weighed so heavily on my heart. I explained how David was identified as a person of small stature. He was told that he was little, and it carried with him. He watered the seeds of shame and guilt and sinned against God. Throughout his years, what was told to him was the most significant impact on his adult life. When he saw Bathsheba, he didn't just sin on that specific day. David's heart was filled with the negative words spoken to him from his childhood. He was a shepherd turned into a king.

He must have felt like a total imposter. When he sent to kill Uriah, Bathsheba's husband, he caused a domino effect, leading to hundreds of deaths. He did it to cover up the sin he committed against Uriah, one of his best soldiers. One thought led him to hurt his people, who he'd sworn to protect. That same thought led him to continue living as if he was still small. His internal war within himself killed a whole army. But one thing God said, after it all was done, that he was a man after his own heart. When I read that, it baffled me. I was like, *God, how can you forgive a sin so great? He harmed innocent people!*

As I look up after my message was nearing its end, I stated that his forgiveness extended to a heart eager to repent. At that moment, I felt in my heart that I should ask two women to hug each other. When they did, the whole church was sobbing. Little did I know, it was the secretary hugging the pastor's wife. The church was grieving because the pastor had an affair with the secretary.

That was the day I felt like it was worth living. I was born to change lives and help others overcome their despair. I romanticized death to be the moment I would experience an overwhelming sense of love that would eliminate the possibility of being alone. It was a lie that I held onto as though it were the truth.

1 Kings 19:4

⁴ But he went a day's journey into the wilderness and came and sat down under a broom tree. And he asked that he might die, saying, "It is enough; now, O Lᴏʀᴅ, take away my life, for I am no better than my fathers." ⁵ And he lay down and slept under a broom

tree. **And behold, an angel touched him and said to him, "Arise and eat."**

Elijah was on the journey God wanted him to be on. He was escaping from the assignment God had for him. When Elijah was about to have deliverance and wanted his life to end, he was tired of fighting. Still, God took that opportunity to feed him, restore his energy, and encourage him to move forward despite how weary he felt. Before the sermon, I would have never known the hurt I was experiencing could be relatable to many. But the seed I was watering, like David, were the words that said I was not worthy.

Feeling unworthy stemmed from the molestation I experienced by my cousins that I hid in my subconscious, not wanting to expose the truth. I thought I was at fault for what had happened. I was not escaping from Jezebel; I ran away from the pain in my chest. A feeling that I didn't deserve God's love. I would talk more about that experience later to emphasize the importance. Please remember that you are worthy of love.

The beautiful experience of love cannot be realized if you do not accept it in your heart. When you recognize your worth, you will acknowledge the love.

Note: I was raised in the church. I spent countless hours in prayer and fasting yet never felt worthy. I was worn down by the weight of guilt, doubt, and frustration within me. We want to be loved, but we will never fully embrace it if we do not know what we are worth. Forgiveness in your heart can open the door to experience God's love in its magnitude. This is true regardless of your religious background, or even if you don't follow a belief system at all. *Please take five minutes, and I dare you to write out why you are worthy!*

5

TO MATTER

Every guy that showed an interest in me was "the one." I would do the death bed test. Can I picture them taking care of me when I am diagnosed with a fatal disease? Did it seem like they would stay or leave? When I would hear their response being ignorant for their age, I would turn the other way. I treated every guy as if they were the one until they were not. It was toxic. I got sick of the cycle of waiting for my prince charming to save this damsel in distress. Being Christian, I did not want my feelings for a man to be too physical because I did not wish lust to be my primary motivation. After years of waiting, I met the man I yearned for...

PRINCE NOT-SO CHARMING

When he walked into the church, he owned it. His eyes were so mesmerizing, but I ignored him. I thought he was handsome but did not want to allow myself to take it further. I was busy with my business, youth presidential duties, and working full-time. I finally came to my own again and felt comfortable in my skin. I did not want anyone to play with my feelings or not be emotionally ready. When I first saw him, it was like his wavy hair had its aura. I mean, he walked into the room. It was like the wind blew through his hair.

Like prince charming arriving on a majestic horse, his eyes were beautiful and captivating. He tried to have conversations with me, but I didn't allow myself to feel. One day, all of that changed. We started texting frequently. I was his youth president, and I took advantage of it to discuss youth events. I wanted to know everything about him. Like a book I could not put down, I wanted to spend every waking hour studying him. I wanted him, and he wanted me. This was refreshing.

I did not plan it for our first date. I didn't even know it *was* the first date. It felt as though it was scheduled without my knowledge. He invited my sister, so I thought little of it. She wasn't interested in being a third wheel. My hair was messy, and I was in sweats. My meal of choice was ribs and fries. Not the best meal on the first date.

While he was ogling me, I had a piece of meat in my teeth. I noticed it when I smiled nervously, with barbecue sauce on my hands. He said he liked that I was myself no matter what setting I was in. I was addicted, kind of like a kid with a pocket full of money in a candy store. I was like glue and stuck to him. I thought it was normal.

You know, like every romantic comedy or Novela, everything happens fast. Is it love without the rush or sense of attachment? I would remember the sounds of his car from afar. It's how I knew he was nearby. I would adjust my clothes and brush my hair. I welcomed him as the love of my life. Talking to him was an escape from reality. It felt great. I felt bombed with his love, and I did not see clearly.

Our dates since then were long talks in my father's backyard, swatting mosquitos: long, eager looks and cute affirmations. I lived for our discussions. It was more fun for me than being surrounded by people in a crowded restaurant. I enjoyed the undivided attention. It felt nice. I felt like I was on top of the world. I'd never had anyone focus on me this way.

We all want to matter to that one person, and when that one person gives us that attention, it makes our day. We strive for others to see us in a way that will make our negative feelings disappear. In all the romantic stories, when the man meets the woman, it is a vivid experience. When Esther met Boaz and acknowledged her for her beautiful traits, it caught her attention. He allowed her positive characteristics to be at the forefront of what he saw, allowing her to feel like she mattered. At least, I would have liked to believe that's how she felt.

I discovered I needed someone to make me feel like I mattered because I didn't feel like I mattered without them. We glorify romantic love and expect it to give our life meaning. We matter when we decide we do. You matter, but you need to believe that you do. Remind yourself of the reasons you matter. If you are waiting for a huge milestone in your life, you will wait forever. Because that moment can arrive, and you will still feel the same.

Note: We matter to God. Despite how our family, friends, and even God sees us, it may not be enough if we think we don't matter. We search for the answers outside when they are really on the inside. We crave a sense of belonging. But we need to create the mold, *not* force ourselves to fit into it. *Please take five minutes, and I dare you to write what it means to matter or belong!*

6

TO BE UNDERSTOOD

The sense of belonging makes us feel like we matter and are understood. This feeling is an enormous need in our hearts. I genuinely believe we join communities, assemblies, sports teams, and even cults to belong. Jim Jones took all the misfits and misunderstood religious strays and took advantage of their vulnerability. When those needs appear to be met, you feel reassurance and love. Have you ever been around a group of people in your life and feel like they don't even know you? As if you were French, while they're Japanese? We think they love us, but they didn't meet us on our terms.

Sometimes we feel like we're the problem. Our love tank feels like it is running on empty. We all want to be understood. We all have some relationship in our life that we think of this way. One of the most influential is the relationship with your family. What impact did your family make in choosing "the one"?

READY OR NOT HERE HE COMES

I have reached a part of my relationship with him where I became enamored. He became my prince charming, and I became his damsel in distress. As I returned home, I was welcomed with unspoken tension. My sister wanted to share a dream with me, and I was not ready to hear it. I was finally happy for an entire day for the first time in a long time, and I wanted nothing to ruin it. She said she had something important to tell me and pleaded with me to hear her out. My sister had a dream about my man and me and that we were fooling around. Also, she saw panties on the floor, and she felt he wanted to fool around with me.

This baffled me. I did not understand what the real problem was. Were they upset that I was happy? I questioned her intentions, as it felt like I was alone in wanting to be satisfied.

I responded in a low, suspicious tone. "Why do you say that? Are you not happy that you want to destroy the happiness of another? Is your marriage not fulfilling enough that you most poke holes where there is not any?" She turned around and refused to retort my series of questions. *Have I not waited long enough to be happy with someone?* The silence was more uncomfortable than the dream she shared.

I walked towards my room and quickly texted him. I left to meet up with him later that evening, although that is not the time I could usually go. But I did it anyway. I needed him. I needed the comfort of his warm embrace to make me feel safe. We agreed to meet up at the diner, and I drove as fast as I could, blasting music to drown out the silence in my mind. I thought a family that loved me would not try to sabotage my happiness. I wanted to talk to him because I wanted to be sure that I was not alone in my feelings.

As I pulled into the parking lot, I noticed he was already there, sitting with a cup of coffee. Usually, he would wait in his car to escort me inside and open my door. I noticed he was speaking to the waitress, laughing together. While I walked inside, I saw her placing her hand on his shoulder, and he put his hand on hers. I did not want to say anything at that moment, afraid I might say more than I meant to. I tried to coach myself. *Girl, you can't take back what you say. You are upset.*

I flung open the twin doors of the diner's entrance and

marched towards them. I looked the waitress up and down while she slowly poured coffee into his already full cup.

"Hola mi Amor," he said, smirking.

"Hi!" I said in a forced, flat tone.

"What is your problem?" he asked angrily.

The anger surprised me.

"Do I not have a right to be upset?" I asked, my voice still raised.

"You just got here. Do not come at me with this jealous crap. Right now, I am having a great day. Do not ruin it for me!" he said.

I stood silent. I did not know how to react to this different side of this man that was charming and kind to me all the time.

"Bebe, Mueneca, Linda..." he said, with a kind of sinister tone.

He laughed at me and mocked my body language.

I wasn't sure if I was overreacting or if my initial response was utterly ordinary.

I responded after a long, awkward pause. "Well, if you won't respect me, I guess I will leave."

He shrugged his shoulders and said, "Oh well."

He leaned back and sipped his hot cup of coffee while never breaking eye contact.

I silently got up and, as I left, I noticed from the corner of my eye that the waitress had gone back to his table and continued to hover over him.

I got back in my car and sped home. I screamed until my voice was hoarse. I could not believe it. My heart was broken. I thought I must be no good to anyone. When will I have someone to love, respect, and accept who I am? *This is freaking ridiculous,* I thought.

When I arrived home, I went through the back door to go unnoticed. As I showered to get ready for bed, I was anxious. Is this what my relationship was like? What do you do when you needed someone and that someone is no longer there? I didn't feel understood by my family, mom, or the church. *What am I left with?* I exclaimed. I fell asleep waiting by my phone. Maybe he would call and apologize for flirting with the waitress. What if he admitted it was wrong?

I woke up several times that night feeling heartbroken that there was no response since the diner. I manically called him at 2:00 a.m.

Two short rings, and he answered. "Hey Baby, what is wrong?"

"Hey," I said in a dry tone.

There was a brief silence.

He seemed normal like nothing had happened. I broke the silence by answering him. "Do you even care about me?"

"Why do you ask that?" He sounded genuinely surprised, as though he didn't know what I was talking about or why I asked.

"Am I creating stuff in my head?" I asked.

He chuckled. "You probably are, but what are you referring to?"

"Did you not want to know if I was coming back or where I went?"

"Listen, this is the difference between you and me."

"What do you mean?" I responded.

"I am a mature adult who does not let stupid stuff get to me. You are just a jealous freak, and I will not entertain that. You need to get over whatever happened to you as a kid and learn that you must start acting like an adult if you want to be in a relationship with an adult."

I was baffled, as I had not seen this side of him. I sat in silence because what do you say to that? Should I be offended, or is being offended immature? At that moment, our seven-year difference felt like a problem that my lack of experience of relationships was the culprit. Maybe I was the common denominator in this equation. I was dumbfounded.

He interrupted the silence. "Baby, you must go to sleep. You must work tomorrow, and I would be grateful if you could sleep. It would help if you did not go to work tired. I love you, and I will see you tomorrow morning."

I was speaking English, but I could not get someone to understand the intentions of my words. I did not have someone to comprehend who I was. If you want to be understood, you must first understand yourself. If your identity is formed loosely on what others say about you, you are not understanding your likes, wants, and even your identity. We sometimes start relationships hoping that we can find ourselves in them, but you must do the work to find yourself. Once we change the story's narrative, others tell us about ourselves; then, we can continue to build the character in who we know ourselves to be.

Note: We can want relationships to work out so badly, despite being harmful to ourselves. We try to force it and keep bending it until it takes the shape we expect. Some relationships are just not worth holding onto. *Take five minutes, and I dare you to write what will make you feel understood!*

7

TO ESCAPE

.

Sometimes, when looking for a partner, we assume they will solve our problems for us. Humanity is complex and profound. We search for a partner who will meet our human needs and hope that partner will be our companion in life. Relationships are not the cure to your voids.

In psychology, we have five human needs that will lead us to be self-actualized. The desire to become the most that one can be. We desire our esteem to be at an all-time high. To be respected through recognition, strength, and freedom. We want to be provided with a sense of love and belonging, friendship, intimacy, family, and a sense of connection. We need to feel safe, which goes hand in hand with personal security, employment, resources, health, and property. Society would have us believe one person will meet all our needs. When we are not whole ourselves, we have nothing to offer a partner. I chose one person to fulfill all my needs, and with that, I was irresponsible. I wanted to have someone who would help me escape from my reality and save me from myself.

In a moment of vulnerability, we seek to fulfill the desires of our hearts. When we put up our blinders, we may do anything to feel loved. The red flags become blurry, and they become gray flags when the need to be loved overpowers the need to be respected. Although love is not manipulation, mind games, and abuse, sometimes we justify the red flags by telling ourselves they're something else.

THE MORNING AFTER

After our 2:00 a.m. phone call, I felt strange. He was angry one moment and sweet the next. His behavior shifted so quickly I questioned if it was happening at all. His lack of acknowledgment baffled me. I ruled out my feelings as ignorant and insecure. I did not want to sleep that night without addressing my concerns, but I had no one to speak with. Telling my family would only confirm their judgment. I decided to make peace with what had happened. I finally had someone that loved me, and I did not want to ruin it with my naive behavior.

I woke up to an uneasy feeling in my chest. I ignored it and got ready for work. Getting an early start, I headed to Mcdonald's to grab some breakfast before I clocked in for work. I drove in the parking lot to find his mustang waiting at the laundry mat by my job. I rubbed my eyes again to make sure I didn't just see things. Maybe this was part of the *novela* where the man apologizes for being a jerk. But no, that was not it. He did not even talk to me about anything else. He looked me up and down and said, "Baby, who are you dressing for?"

"No one." I reluctantly made eye contact, afraid I would get lost in his eyes.

We pulled into the laundry mat, and he shifted to being the charming man I that was endearing. In front of the laundry mat was a McDonald's. It was the only thing open at 5:00 a.m., so that's where we ordered. I was tired, and my eyes burned. I had mustered the strength to wake up early, to see my handsome prince and make amends.

As we waited for our order, we locked eyes while I nervously played with the rim of my cup of hot chocolate. He whispered sweet nothings in my ear, and it made all the hairs on my body stand on end. At that moment, he could do no wrong. He shifted his foot forward, and I did the same until both of our feet met. My cheeks grew hot, and I was flustered. I did not want to acknowledge the nervous tension, as I'd never had any level of intimacy with another man.

As I got closer to him, he shivered, and I gently caressed the side of his cheek. That single touch made me feel empowered, desired, and loved. I watched as this 6'0" ft man melted before me. I felt like I could finally love and be loved. This pure and gentle moment contrasted the battle of the conflicting thoughts from the night before. I quickly surrendered my anger and accepted that I was the problem.

I idolized the concept of falling in love with this reckless ideation of what he desired. Too many times, I abandoned my gut feeling when something was wrong. I identified these messages as the guide of the Holy Spirit. I ignored his whispers in my soul, trying to show me the red flags. The controlling behavior that signaled a toxic relationship was dismissed because of my desire to feel loved by this man. Physically, he portrayed the attributes of the love of my life.

I wanted to escape from myself, from feeling like the only way to redemption was in the arms of a man. I had a lifelong internal conflict I believed a man could solve.

Psalm 142:7

Bring my soul out of prison that I may praise thy name: the righteous shall compass me about; for thou shalt deal bountifully with me.

David, during that time, was in a cave, not in prison, hiding from Saul. David was afraid because Saul attempted to kill him many times. He was experiencing physical captivity and a spiritual one. He prayed for God to free his *soul* out of prison. We often find ourselves in this position, and we may think that our solution is the best one.

Note: Do you feel that experiencing a romantic form of love would suffice the vacancy in your heart? *Please take five minutes, and I dare you to write what you are trying to escape from and how that influences your ability to love!*

8

TO BE SOMEONE'S WORLD

I went from running away from my problems to running into his arms. I was escaping into someone else's world. Did I finally find the one? He had been the man who could cover my wounds and heal the hurt. I was his world. We were always on the phone talking to each other when we were not physically together. He saw me. He heard me. The only thing I ever wanted. I finally wasn't someone's afterthought. I thought his love was like...

1 Corinthians 13

[4] Love is patient. Love is kind. It does not envy, and it does not boast. It is not proud. [5] It does not dishonor others, is not self-seeking, is not easily angered, and keeps no record of wrongs. [6] Love does not delight in evil but rejoices with the truth. [7] It always protects, always trusts, always hopes, always perseveres. [8] Love never fails.

I came to realize that the need to be in someone's world was causing me to wear blinders. Another thing we crave is the need for importance. We all want to be important to our family or the world. That is why some pursue fame so aggressively. We are trying to please this invisible crowd, even though many of them are naysayers. That is why so many kids, from middle school through high school, do things they don't want to do, just to gain approval. As part of that sense of belonging, I felt I needed to get married. I wanted to be important and part of someone's world.

I DO, OR I DON'T

We were preparing for a big event with the youth group, and my sister, being the leader, was organizing a talent show. This show would include singing and small performances. I was eager to be a part of it, as I always enjoyed the preaching portion. He would sing, and I was told my portion of the talent show would be coming up soon. I became impatient when I thought I lost my place. As I waited, I noticed he was just as nervous, and I was teasing him about being scared. When my turn came, I preached from the depths of my soul about David, how he was always getting into trouble with God, and how he was still defined as a man after God's heart. We can get into trouble, but that doesn't mean we lose his heart—his love for us.

As I concluded, I realized his part was coming soon. He sang, and it was *his favorite* song. I blushed when I realized everyone was staring back at me. He stopped singing and began a speech in the middle of the song. "Beatrice, you are the woman I always prayed for..." My eyes were fixed on him, and the whole room became silent and blurry. Walking closer to me, he got on one knee. "Will you marry me?" he asks. I grinned so hard my ears hurt. I kissed him before I could utter a word. When I looked up, I noticed everyone applauding and hollering.

I was excited but based on all the soap operas and the romantic comedies I had watched, it did not feel the way I thought it would. I assumed my years of insecurities would vanish once the world knew my worth. That all my doubts about him would become void. I felt known for those twenty minutes, but I didn't even know myself. I was doing what I thought was right. I turned around and eagerly accepted. That was the correct response, right? When someone is offering their world, shouldn't you take it? It seems only gracious to accept. What a world it was...

I had to prove to this invisible audience they were wrong. The audience was shame and guilt, and they were always loud in the VIP section.

1 Samuel 1 6-8

6 Because the LORD had closed Hannah's womb, her rival kept provoking her to irritate her. 7 This went on year after year. Whenever Hannah went up to the house of the LORD, her rival provoked her till she wept and would not eat. Her husband Elkanah would say to her,

"Hannah, why are you weeping? Why don't you eat? Why are you downhearted? Don't I mean more to you than ten sons?"

Hannah was desperate for a baby. Hannah wanted the ability to be a mother. Although I never realized the intensity of my want over my need, I felt this was the proper thing to do. I remembered when moments like, "In her bitter distress, Hannah prayed to the Lord and wept with many tears," that I was just like her. Ever since I was nine years old, I prayed for a man to heal my hurt and love me. When speaking to God, there were times that my prayers to have a life partner became as loud as Hannah's sobbing.

The Sunday after the engagement, we arrived at church. We were the couple ushered into the church with celebratory greetings, and many hugged and even cried when they saw my ring. They were so eager to see me arrive at this point in my life. This was my first boyfriend, and I was determined he would be my last. Quickly, after the preaching was over, the pastor's wife asked if she could pray. I accepted the offer and grabbed him by the arm. She said she felt this union was from God. But as she uttered those words, my soul quickly screamed. *What if he tries to kill me?* I did not understand why a rush of doubt flooded my mind as she prayed. This was the moment I was waiting eagerly. I should have been more confident, but everything within me contradicted her prayer.

Note: Do not silence the voice that guides you. Some refer to this as your "gut feeling." Allowing your inner voice to guide you is essential. If you silence that voice, you are walking a dangerous path. It always looks out for your well-being. Sometimes the opinions of others can be paralyzing. If you are a people pleaser, this one is tough. Sometimes, what we suspected all along is the answer. The need to appease others and to feel validated can consume you and may not allow you to consider your life choices. *Please take five minutes, and I dare you to write what will make you feel known, important and seen.*

9

TO FEEL WANTED

We all want to feel wanted, desired, and upheld as a vision of beauty. We want to be embraced in our imperfections. We want to feel the touch that validates those emotions and the looks that warm our souls. Wanting to be desired by your partner is perfectly normal. Sometimes we place ourselves in a position where their desire may not be the same as ours. It's hard because when you do not feel desired by your partner, it bothers you. I wanted to feel beautiful in his arms and hoped he would make me feel gorgeous, despite my physical imperfections.

SIX MONTHS AFTER

He caressed me with a gentle touch that made my hair stand on end. He kissed me slowly, and his lips were so supple. He moved my hair away from my face and our eyes locked. I felt desired and treasured, as though my body was gold. I removed my clothes, and he was eager to have me. I wanted this. I wanted it to be like a scene from a soap opera, where the man only wanted one woman and no one else. To be desired, without being compared to other women.

Our honeymoon started with small kisses and gentle caressing in the shower. I anticipated the pleasure. After a few minutes of stimulation, he finished, but it disappointed him that I did not orgasm. I never knew what that was like experiencing an orgasm. I stared at him, waiting for the magic to happen. I wanted to keep trying because this was what everyone talked about, and indeed, they couldn't be wrong.

He laid beside me and rested. I turned over and caressed his inner thigh, but he quickly removed my hand.

"Is this why you got married?" he asked.

"One of the reasons," I said.

"Can we buy a movie instead?"

He wanted our honeymoon experience to be more than sex. We watched the film, and he fell asleep, but I was so disappointed. I wanted to keep trying and wanted to achieve an orgasm, as he said. Throughout the night, he complained about pain, and I heard him crying. I tried to help him, but I did not understand what was wrong because, frankly, I did not know what kind of pain he was feeling. Until just then, I was only aware of a bit of back pain he had previously. I spun to my side and whispered in my heart, *was this what I waited for my whole virgin life?*

I felt like a disgusting predator for wanting sex, and I tossed and turned the entire night. He woke me up, tears flooding his pillow. He said it bothered him we couldn't have satisfying sex. At least, not the way he wanted.

I still have no idea if he felt this pain or how much of it there was. I felt like a prostitute and needed to repent for being with my husband. He made me feel shame for wanting to be wanted. I spent my entire life waiting to discover what it was like to be with someone. I felt rejected for the rest of the honeymoon and felt my body wasn't enough to please him. He did not want to leave the hotel room for the whole honeymoon. I worried my future would be like this. I had to beg to be desired.

In the story of Samson and Delilah, she didn't understand what gave him strength. She talked him into releasing the secret. She spent countless attempts to find out what would make him break. His strength was his locks, and his weakness was his desire. Why else would he be tempted by Delilah if not for this desire? A temptation you face is merely a desire that may not serve you.

Like Samson, over time, I became mentally weak to his ability to convince me to try new things. A few months after we wed, we decided to make love one night. But he had a new condition. He wanted to fantasize about his brother's girlfriend while we did it. He wanted me to scream and speak the way she spoke. I didn't understand.

"Am I not enough for you?" I asked.

"If you don't do it, I can get someone else who will." he retorted

Fighting back the tears, I agreed to this role-play. Then, he asked me to describe her body.

I hesitated again. "Can't we role-play as someone we don't know?" I asked.

He insisted. "I want this. I need this."

I continued the role-playing and saw the pleasure it gave him.

I heard a whisper in my soul.

Philippians 4:8

Finally, brothers and sisters, whatever is true, whatever is noble, whatever is right, whatever is pure, whatever is lovely, whatever is admirable—if anything is excellent or praiseworthy—think about such things.

My soul hurt, and I immediately regretted agreeing to do it. I had opened a door that would become difficult to shut. The embedded religious dogmas shaped me to believe that God's love was not technically unconditional. That he was only a God of wrath and that being loved came with a set of unreachable expectations. At that moment, I felt God's love, so gentle and kind. A love I had never encountered before. I wanted to shed my skin, as I no longer felt comfortable in it. This would become one of many countless sexual experiences I'd wish I hadn't been involved in.

Hebrews 13:4

Let marriage be held in honor among all, and let the marriage bed be undefiled, for God will judge the sexually immoral and adulterous.

Note: As a partner, we feel pressured to meet the desires of the person we love. It is hard to say no when you think you may hurt them. We want to give everything to them. Sometimes we do not desire the same things sexually, and some experiences can trigger traumas you fought hard to overcome. Sex is an integral part of a relationship, but it is hard to balance when your relationship with sex becomes unhealthy. Sex is a part of love. It is one of the ways we feel wanted and desired. *Please take five minutes, and I dare you to write what will make you feel wanted!*

10

TO FEEL SAFE

When you get married to someone, you carry their struggles and pain. We had our good and bad days, but there were many moments where the bad would overwhelm the good, and it was becoming difficult to see the good anymore. His health was getting worse, and we already had two babies. Between his appointments and my two infants, I was always exhausted. But what was there to complain? This was married life, right?

One day, there came a turning point in our marriage. It was cold out. It was a lazy Sunday morning, and I wanted to sleep. I was exhausted by being up all night with the girls, and he encouraged me to stay in bed. He reassured me he would make some coffee. As I lay in bed, I was anxious. There was a chilly breeze, and I wanted to find out where the direction of the breeze was. It was January on a cold winter morning, and I had the heater turned on. I went to check the heater, and I heard a noise. The front door cracked open, and my husband stared at the neighbor's yard. He was naked and fully erected; there was proof of his orgasm dripping down his leg. I was so shocked and disturbed.

I didn't understand at all what was happening. There was no one awake, and it was negative thirty degrees outside. I could not believe my eyes and almost questioned if I was dreaming.

"Why..." I asked, my voice cracking.

He spun around, surprised I was up and that he'd been caught. He sprinted to the reclining chair inside. I was overwhelmed by shock as if the man I married was removing another mask I did not know he'd been wearing.

When he finally answered, he only offered one explanation: "*She* made me do it."

I kept asking who "she" was. There was no one else around. But something from this moment seemed too familiar. This moment helped to explain why I married this man. It was as though my traumatized inner child was forced to the surface. It took me to the moment I refused to re-live.

When I was a kid, my cousin and his sister would corner me, touching my body and fingering me when no one was around. I was involved in a relationship that provoked shame. I realized I married the "normal" man I thought I deserved. The motto boys will be boys echoed in my head. I could remember my name being called from the basement, beckoning me to watch my cousin masturbate. The countless times in the church van, he fingered me. I married the man I *thought* I deserved. Two become one, and it came full circle. Does shame count?

Job's wife was judged for wanting out. Was this the same? I was convinced that it wasn't abuse because my cousin was my age. I thought because of his age that he did not know any better. Am I to blame because I froze every time it happened? I should have made him stop.

The broken little girl inside me tried to marry what I could not fix as a child. I was consumed by guilt because I never told anyone about my cousin as a kid. I decided that I must have deserved this. This man I married was my deserved punishment for my silence and shame from all these years. I should have seen the signs, but I was blind to them because this was just the sort of sexual perversion I thought I deserved.

I saw him differently from that moment forward, but he tried to pretend it never happened. Why did I feel bad for looking at him differently? He was struggling. "In sickness and health," right? His unexplained absences for countless hours at night made sense now. He wanted to expose himself in public. It crippled my nights with worries. What if he did that in front of someone who would attack him? What if he did it in front of a child? What if...

You know, the cruelest lie the devil can tell you is that you are alone. One verse that tugs at my soul is this one:

Joshua 1:9
Be strong. Be brave. Be fearless. You are never alone.

I know now that I am not alone. Many of us have experienced abuse as a child, and we face similar experiences as adults. The 2006 *World Report on Violence against Children* provided estimates that, in 2002, approximately 150 million girls and 73 million boys were subject to sexual abuse worldwide. This would include 1.2 million trafficked children and 1.8 million exploited through prostitution or pornography. I believe there is a correlation between the two, and the evidence supports this. Many women become part of a violent domestic relationship, not because they deserve it, but because these experiences have convinced us we do.

You are not alone. There is a beauty in knowing that you are not alone; a man, or woman who has suffered abuse, no longer has to feel alone. Knowing this information can help you survive from what has been done to you. There is a way out.

We must also be careful if we choose to stay in a relationship because we can save the man or change him. If we are not healed ourselves, it is unwise to enter a relationship to heal someone else.

Proverbs 4:23

Above all else, guard your heart, for everything you do flows from it. You deserve to live your life in peace, love, and harmony. Choose you in midst of the hurt. Protect your heart, you only have one.

Note: Surround yourself with people that make you feel safe. Create a support system to heal from any trauma you may have faced. If you have a troubled soul, you cannot think clearly to love wisely. *Please take five minutes, and I dare you to write what will help you feel safe to love again!*

11

TO BE HELD

I had reached a point in the relationship where I felt overwhelmed and did not know how to handle a man with inappropriate sexual urges. I felt like a prisoner in a marriage I brought on myself. I felt stuck because this man saw nothing wrong with his behavior. There is no need to change if you see nothing wrong with what you are doing, right? I was coping with this internally, out of fear of putting my loved ones and myself in harm's way. I didn't have friends to run to because I lost them all, because of worrying about how his behavior might show up in public. I didn't tell my family because I was more afraid of the "I told you so" than leaving. How could I face them? Their belief that I was the stupid little sister had come true, right? I wanted to be held and told that this was just a nightmare and it was just my imagination.

GOODBYE PEACE

I was saying goodbye to my uncle that had just passed. But death was so apparent, not only at the funeral but in the stares from my family. Besides the grief, I felt like no one wanted to get near me. It was as if they knew something but did not want to tell me.

I approached my mom.

"We are at a funeral, and my sisters act as if I did something wrong to them. What did I do? I cannot stand the uncomfortable silence. What is going on?" I pleaded.

My mom hesitated. "I have something to tell you..."

"I want to know!" I screamed.

"This isn't the time or the place to tell you," she said.

"Ma, tell me!"

I was desperate. I had a horrible feeling. Part of me knew what she was about to say, but I wanted to hear it from her mouth.

"I'll tell you another time," she insisted.

"I will leave right now if you don't tell me," I begged, crying. I couldn't bear waiting for another second. I felt like vomiting and running and screaming all at once.

"Okay, Mami, your sister well... your sister..."

"What MA? What about my sister?"

"Your husband..." She seemed concerned as she saw him in the corner of the room.

"What about him, Ma?"

"Your husband did something to your sister, and I think you should hear it from her directly."

After telling her we'd meet at the burial site, I ran to the car, fuming about the whole situation.

Once there, I was able to speak with my sister.

"What happened?" I asked.

She began crying. "I swear, I didn't do anything!"

"What? Tell me. I want to know! Please stop playing with my feelings."

She continued crying. "All I want to tell you for right now is that he sexually harassed me, and I will call you later to tell you more. I can't talk about it now."

I ran back to my car, where he was waiting for me. The father of my children. The love of my life. I stayed silent, but there was a storm brewing inside of me.

"What happened?" he asked.

"What?" I asked in response.

"Tell me!"

I stood silent.

I wanted to confront him, but not when we were in the car. I felt he would get angry like he always did and use the car as a weapon to threaten me.

"Tell me! What did your lying family say I did now?"

He knew this was coming.

He never wanted me to bury my uncle, and he never wanted me to see my family. He mentioned it to me that same morning. He said my sisters were too promiscuous, and that's why they were a terrible influence on our daughters.

"You idiot, what did you do?" I screamed. "You are guilty of something, and you know it. What did you do?"

He was silent.

"What did you do?" I repeated.

He shouted back and started speeding dangerously. We almost crashed into a truck that got too close. Then he swerved past it and narrowly missed a tiny red car.

"See what I can do?" he taunted. His green eyes seemed to turn black, and his pupils were huge, the vein in his neck bulging. "I could kill you," he said. "I can kill you first and make the girls watch. Then, I'll kill myself. Or if your family wants to say anything else, I'll kill them in a way no one would ever find out about."

I was quiet until we arrived home. I wanted to be held. I felt like I was living the part of the soap opera where I would watch with anxiety, terrified of what the villain was about to do... except the villain was the man the damsel fell in love.

My soul was quivering. Did I deserve this?

Romans 8:27

And we know that in all things, God works for the good of those who love him, who have been called according to his purpose.

Psalm 91:1-2

Whoever dwells in the shelter of the Most High will rest in the shadow of the Almighty. I will say of the LORD, "He is my refuge and my fortress,

   my God, in whom I trust."

I could have quoted all the verses I memorized as a girl. I could have rebuked him in God's name. But, at that moment, I feared for the well-being of my girls, my family, and myself. I was silent.

Note: The moment the person we love betrays us, we can feel shocked. Our expectations of them fall short, and we are disappointed. Looking back, I was the Judas to myself and thought I deserved a man like this. I am not responsible for his actions, but I *am* accountable for my decisions. I sold my love for a few kisses and empty promises to a man who couldn't afford it because he did not have love to give. *Please take five minutes, and I dare you to write what will make you feel welcomed, supported, and on the path to healing!*

12

TO BE ENOUGH

That was the last straw. I couldn't do it anymore. A loud, toxic voice in my head had been repeating the same line: You are not enough. His actions made it feel like a self-fulfilling prophecy. I told myself I was not enough. Therefore, I wasn't.

"You are not woman enough."

"You are not skinny enough."

"You are not generous enough."

"You are not pretty enough."

"You are not smart enough."

Enough. I no longer wanted to be defined by a set of standards created by society, family, and friends. The man who promised to love and protect me became the same person I needed protection from. I came back home and tried to minimize the damage. I was consumed by what I lacked in the relationship that I neglected to consider what was being provided. I focused on healing him; I did not acknowledge my need for healing. His inability to love was not my responsibility. His inability to see his wrongdoing was also not my responsibility.

We continued the conversation on the safer ground—our home. I told him about everything that was said to me, and he denied it. He didn't even want to talk about it anymore. I was that wife—the secret keeper. But sometimes, keeping those secrets can lead to becoming harmful to others. Not only yourself. We all have those moments where enough is enough. And that was mine. I can not imagine a world where my daughters would label a toxic relationship as a loving one.

I was like the people of Israel. The people of Israel took forty years for a journey that should have taken them twenty-two days. God tried to rescue me from this metaphorical land. I was like the people when they traveled to Marah, where they found bitter water. God sweetened the water for them, gave them some laws, and promised to be their healer in Exodus 15:23-26.

It took me twenty-seven years for a journey that could have been shorter. I realized I was enough when I decided to end the self-hate, comparing myself to others and people-pleasing.

After I accepted the truth, I didn't know how to fix such an awful situation. Until death do us part? In sickness and in health?

I prayed there was a way to move on and make my

family whole again. We planned on having a family meeting to provide healing. As I waited for that Thursday to come, I could not sleep. I would stare at him while he was asleep, hoping to understand the betrayal. I wanted to know how I missed this abuse. I slept roughly thirty minutes for the entire week and could eat nothing because of how disgusted I felt. I had never felt my heart torn this way.

I loved that man, but he did not love me back. I would never be enough for a man who did not know how to love. As the days drew closer to our family meeting, I found myself trusting him less and less. The echoes in my mind of the threat of him killing me and me were constant torture. I knew if I had to get out, I had to make sure I was smart about it.

I made him park outside my job parking lot. I worked at a government job, so there was surveillance. I knew my girls would've always been safe with police on the premises. He had the option to come clean-or go to a psych ward to get evaluated. His behavior was perverse and out of control. A couple of months before, he had been accused of doing the same thing. Except he said, it was a misunderstanding. As naive as I was, I believed him.

Thursday came, and my family arrived at my house. My sister read a letter to him, and he passively denied everything that she accused him of. His response was only thanking her for bringing up things he must've forgotten.

There was no repentance and no apologies. There was no acknowledgment of his behavior.

I gave him an ultimatum: To voluntarily check himself in for treatment or go to the police. He chose treatment. He went in willingly, and the behavioral unit picked him up later that night. When I visited him, he still pretended to have Parkinson's disease, jerked around, and stuttered. I was ashamed. And he was already fooling around with a patient in the same ward! Enough was enough.

His recovery was a joke to him, and to get the proper help, you need to accept something is wrong. I ran home, grabbed my belongings, and then went to court and filed a restraining order. I could not have my children around this man any longer. My daughters are my world, and I couldn't expose them to this kind of risk.

Your experiences were never meant to break you but to strengthen you. I chose to give up my vulnerability and my virginity. He betrayed me so profoundly that I thought my soul would collapse. If you find yourself in this same situation, I urge you to leave metaphorical Egypt. Get out of the relationship that holds you captive with lies and empty promises. If they say they love you, but their action contradicts those words, get out. If you are experiencing their abuse and manipulation, get out of Egypt. You can't change them, and you can't make them love you.

Fear can be crippling, especially when you are thinking of leaving an abusive relationship. One promise, I held onto for strength:

. . .

Exodus 3:11-12a

But Moses said to God, "Who am I that I should go to Pharaoh and bring the Israelites out of Egypt?" And God said, "I will be with you..."

Note: You are not to blame for the abuse you experience. You did not make your abuser do it. They are responsible for the harsh words, the manipulation, the sexual control, and everything else. You are worthy of transitioning from being a victim to healing as a survivor. You are strong enough to leave—set boundaries. Money should not be your crutch or the lack thereof. Being in a shelter or "imposing" on a family member is a better option than not knowing if you will wake up the next day or fearing for the safety of your children.

You will not stay afraid. There will be better days. Remember that you will be uncomfortable for a while, but you must be. Discomfort provokes change. Your mindset, belief systems, and habits didn't serve you before, so you need to change them. You need to get out of Egypt. What is enough for you? And what will make you feel enough? *Please take five minutes, and I dare you to write five reasons you are enough!*

13

TO HEAL

Love can be found in many different places, and you cannot even accept the Love of God if you do not think you are worth loving. I decided to live again. Previously, I had never wanted to see the age of thirty. My plan, since I was young, was to die young. I thought that when I died, I would finally feel loved. I was desperate for help and made the life-changing decision to seek professional help. I did not realize how much self-hatred I held in my heart until my therapist told me to look in the mirror to forgive myself.

When I looked in the mirror, I was too ashamed to look at the person I betrayed time and time again. I was physically sick to my stomach, looking back at the woman I had become. I was different, same big round eyes, small lips, pronounced nose, and thick eyebrows, but there was that look in my eye. My eyes no longer had that shine that eluded happiness.

I needed to forgive myself. I wanted to live again. I wanted to enjoy the taste of my favorite pizza. I wanted to enjoy my children's smiles. To walk outside and breathe in the peaceful air God gave us.

I had created a vision board, and I decided to dream again. To wake up and aspire to better myself, grow, learn and smile again. I deserved it. In the past, I thought I didn't. I told myself it wasn't worth the fight because I hoped God would take me away to end all the pain. I thought this constant heartache would end once he came and saved me. Shortly after, I received a court-cited invitation to attend a parenting class. It baffled me that I was expected to take part in this. I was the victim!

PARENTING, RIGHT?

There I was, sitting in this chair. Typically, classrooms are synonymous with boredom and exhaustion. At least, they were for me! Going to school was not fun for me growing up, except maybe college. Today felt like a stepping stool for change. Sounds weird, right? But you know there are days you sense a change coming. I never imagined I'd pay a measly $35 for a life-changing shift in my reality! What seemed like it would be torture turned out to be spring cleaning for my soul. It was an appointment for a redirection.

This teacher was quirky, silly, and downright inspirational. She seemed like a redheaded 78-year-old version of me. Let's call her Mrs. Frizzle. The teacher had Christmas tree light earrings and a necklace bigger than she was and her loud, joyous laughter echoed in this small room of anxious parents. She saw the sadness in each one of us.

After signing us all in her little sign-in book and briefly going over the rules, she began the class.

"What is your purpose here on earth?" she asked.

That question hit us like a splash of ice-cold water on a hot day. Nearly every one began to tear up. As she continued to speak, it was as if my soul was breaking free. Free of the weight of hurt that had become a burden in my heart. She reaffirmed that we are not alone. We are not unique to this pain, and it isn't forever. I had heard these words before in the church.

My belief system reminded me that God is always here with me, but I admit I did not feel that way. I questioned God and his role in my life. I asked him, as a father, why would He allow his daughter that he says he loves to suffer this pain. Mrs. Frizzle's words seemed to bring healing like I hadn't experienced before. She was like a nurse cleaning up an old wound. As if those words were just for me. She reminded us that our love for our spouse doesn't need to burden our children. Loving them can be an individual experience.

Being parents, you forget. That the DNA of your children is split fifty-fifty, and the creation of your children came from the love between the two of you. It is something I would have to remind myself. Children are not property. They are living, breathing humans like us. They are not bait to make your spouse do whatever you want them to do. They observe and mimic our feelings and behavior. They are a part of us, no matter what. Learn one thing: Don't make it about yourself and your bad experience. Love yourself despite it all, and maybe you will love again.

You may be the wronged parent. But that doesn't mean you have no role to play in the recovery process. Your children will reflect the way you love yourself. We need to seek help if we have a hard time confronting the pain. We must put our ego aside to improve ourselves. The parenting class may have been a requirement, but I used it as an opportunity to grow. Let the negative go. The pain. The anger. The past. If your upbringing caused you to suffer, you could give your children the opportunity to have a healthy parent, and you would not have to pass that pain to them. Break that cycle! It was not your fault, but we must grow from the place of anguish we are in, or we will never be free of it.

Note: *He meant everything for our good.* "Good" sounds like a terrible adjective to use considering the trauma we've faced, but there is a bigger picture we need to see. Your losses and your wins speak volumes to everyone around you. One day, you can share your story to save someone else! *Please take five minutes, and I dare you to write what you need to heal. You can live again and love beyond just a romantic relationship.*

14

TO BE SAVED

I felt as though my heart filled with layers of scars. I was a prisoner to my hurt. However, despite my initial response, the parenting class had proven to help open my heart again. To allow God in, which I was so reluctant to do before. I needed to wipe my slate clean; this class helped me take that decisive step in the right direction. I needed to find the key, to unlock the pain of this lonely heart. I was in a prison of despair and loneliness.

I'd locked myself in a prison that I'd always had the key.

Psalm 142:7

Bring my soul out of prison, that I may praise thy name: the righteous shall compass me about; for thou shalt deal bountifully with me.

· · ·

I felt shame, guilt, unworthiness, despair, and body image issues that had chased me for years. I could relate to David in this. He ran away from Saul, but he was not in a physical prison. There were threats against his life. His relationship with Saul was one he could not fathom would end so horribly. His best friend Jonathan was like a brother to him and was so close that I can only imagine it felt as if it was his father that was trying to kill him. It hurts the most when we are hurt by the ones we love. He was in a cave, and although he was King, he could have fixed the situation. He knew how. But he couldn't because you are bound to a place of conflict within yourself when you love someone that hurts you.

The years I waited to fall in love, the idea of love made me race to the altar. Even Christ was offering His love, and I could not accept it. My definition of self-worth held me captive. You can never love with open arms if you do not know how to love yourself. It may be the purest form of love, but we can't experience it if we cannot accept it. You should believe you're worthy. The entanglement of negativity should not convince you that you are unworthy of love.

Those threats haunted me. The memories of him spending hours on the dark web and making crazy claims about his past with pride in his eyes.

"I almost killed a guy in Massachusetts. I mean, I think I did," he once bragged, with a smile on his face.

He held that threat as a badge of honor. I took those

words as promises. One of the few promises he made I thought he would keep. The echoes of that loud car haunted me. Every time I hear a car like that passing by, it reminds me of that promise he made to me. To love, to hold, to protect, to kill, and to manipulate. They'd merged into one, and I didn't know what to believe. This wasn't the man I thought I married. This was a monster. I had just chosen not to see it.

The worst feeling you can have is to fear, with every fiber of your being, someone you loved. Our relationship was not what I thought it was. My heart was broken, and my mind trapped, trying to see the moment that my hero became the villain.

What do I do with this love? Was this love in vain? Did I waste four years of my life with someone that never cherished my passion and heart? I gave him everything: my purity, my morals, my self-respect, and my peace. I felt like a piece of me was missing.

One thing that is rarely mentioned is that the hard part of leaving is often the pain in the aftermath. If you leave a manipulative or abusive relationship, you are left with insecurities and lacking a feeling of safety. You question everyone and everything around you.

My foundation of what I thought was love was shaken to the core. But you know what? It had to be. This pain was necessary. Every tear was essential in creating the person I needed to be. What did not serve me had to be left behind, along with the relationship. I decided to see it as a bad experience and not a bad life.

That day I surrendered my all: the false expectations, the hurt, the past, and anguish. I was so overwhelmed with not finding a job, not providing, not being enough, and questioning my worth that I sometimes felt suicidal. It was different this time. I felt like I failed my daughters and deserved a better mother, home, and resources. I rationalized this for so long that it made sense.

I read the news and saw the story of a preacher who had killed himself. The article explained the reason. He dealt with suicidal ideations. It upset me because once you interpret it as the correct way of thinking, it only feeds into the idea. This article troubled my soul, and I fell asleep with tears.

I shared this article on Facebook, and in the post, I wrote that God will always meet you halfway, and you don't need to end your life. I could not find a valid excuse to leave my children without a mother, significantly when their father could not raise them with his troubled mind. I prayed to God that I needed his love, and I needed him to meet me halfway because I was too tired to go the rest of the distance. I pleaded with God and asked him to please give me an appointment with faith because I need to know that he was hearing me. I felt God speak to my heart as though he heard me.

I decided I needed to find a way out of this vicious mental cycle. The next day was Sunday, and I felt in my heart that I needed to attend a local church, hoping to hear something that would enlighten my soul. The pastor that day was preaching on true love. I was interested because my heartfelt was robbed of love. He said that our idea of love could be based on how we receive God's Love.

God is a gentleman and will never force someone to accept him. I silently prayed for God to show me the part of the message that was meant for me. As the preaching went on, he explained we misplace our love with the expectation of God's Love. That is why we sometimes expect love from others, and they fall short. I wanted to cry. I had not heard a message so fitting and at such a perfect time.

The preacher stepped to the alter and said, "God wants me to tell you today that he wants to meet you halfway. If your heart is troubled, come to the altar to receive the rest from him."

I saw those words as a sign that he was speaking to me. Desperate for answers, I walked toward the altar. I looked around to see if I was the only one who did. I looked up, expecting the pastor to pray for me, but he did not move from the pulpit. I bowed my head and felt a hand on my shoulder, then heard a voice from behind me.

"Hello, I am Faith. How are you feeling?" Her eyes radiated peace, love, and understanding. I instantly cried as she said, today is your day. She prayed so God can heal me from the painful past I have endured. I had never met this woman. I had never visited this church before. I was angry with God, but he still loved me. Such a time as this, God loved me.

I felt the pain in my chest and the weight of the sins I thought I carried for my husband. God works in ways we can not comprehend. Sometimes, when we decide to surrender to what he desires for us, we can accept what we deserve. I was finally saved by the hero I never received because I never thought I deserved his salvation.

1 Corinthians 13:8
Love never fails.

Note: I finally accepted His love when I met him halfway. We must meet him halfway. God is a gentleman. He knocks at your door, but you must invite him in. And with his love comes healing and forgiveness. *Please take five minutes, and I dare you to write what you need in your life to be saved!*

15

YOU ARE LOVED

If I told you that you are loved, would you believe me? You are noticed, cared for beyond human comprehension. Your physical appearance does not change the quality of God's love. But we can not ignore that we try to find ourselves in a person and sometimes lose ourselves in our romantic relationships. We sometimes give without receiving anything in return, and we run on empty. I have discovered that my flawed mindset was to start a relationship with the expectation of making someone else complete and needing them to complete me. I came into the relationship half-empty, with half of my identity formed. Half of my wants and needs were developed, and I expected this one person to fix everything else for me. There are so many layers to us. We were made in the image of God. A testimony I heard several years back started with a story about a man having a vision that he went to heaven and saw God, and the angels were standing in line to see Him too.

In that line, there were many angels, and they were in awe because no matter how many times they saw his face, they continued to see another beautiful side of God. All the better that we were created in his image. We are complex. We never stop learning more about ourselves. We continue to grow and discover our entire lives. We should not select a person to spend our whole life based on superficial standards or selfish needs. We should desire to grow and love ourselves in order to have something to offer in the relationship, beyond sex, money, and stability.

The life partner you should pursue should understand that you will *add* to their lives. They should not compromise your moral integrity, and they should have a foundation of friendship. They should have a mindset of growth and understanding that you will be a team. In this fundamental truth, you can feel loved. We universally seek to be cared for, noticed, worthy, to matter, to be understood, to escape, to be someone's world, to be wanted, to feel safe, to be held, to be enough, to find healing, and to be saved.

You are loved: "You are loved beyond measure." Ephesians 3:19 That not despite your flaws but because you have them you are loved. So much so when Just before Jesus died, He cried out in Aramaic, quoting Psalm 22:1, "My God, My God, why have You forsaken Me?" Suddenly, Jesus cried out, "Eli, Eli, lama sabachthani?" That is the most explicit depiction of loneliness and how he felt he still made the sacrifice.

You are cared for: Matthew 18:12 How think ye? If a man has a hundred sheep and one of them be gone astray, doth he does not leave the ninety and nine, and goeth into the mountains and seeketh that which is gone astray?

You are noticed: 1 Samuel 16:7, But the LORD said to Samuel, "Do not look on his appearance or the height of his stature, because I have rejected him. For the LORD sees not as man sees man looks on the outward appearance, but the LORD looks on the heart."

You are worthy. Romans 5:8, But God shows his love for us in that while we were still sinners, Christ died for us.

You do matter. "I am your Creator. You were in my care even before you were born." Isaiah 44:2a

You are understood. Jeremiah 33:3 Call to me, and I will answer you and tell you great and unsearchable things you do not know.

. . .

You have somewhere to escape to Psalm 91:7 A thousand may fall at your side, ten thousand at your right hand, but it will not come near you.

You are someone's world: John 3:16 For God so loved the world.

You are wanted: John 15:16 You did not choose me, but I chose you and appointed you that you should go and bear fruit and that your fruit should abide, so that whatever you ask the Father in my name, he may give it to you.

You can feel safe: When you pass through the waters, I will be with you; and through the rivers, they shall not overwhelm you; when you walk through the fire, you shall not be burned, and the flame shall not consume you. Isaiah 43.2

You can be held: Isaiah 49:16 Behold, I have engraved you on the palms of my hands; your walls are continually before me.

You are enough: Psalm 139: 13 For You formed my inmost being. You knit me together in my mother's womb. 14 I praise You, for I am fearfully and wonderfully made. Marvelous are Your works, and I know this very well.

You can heal: Peter tells us that "Love covers a multitude of sins" (1Peter 4:8). He echoes the proverb, "Hatred stirs up strife, but love covers all sins" (Proverbs 10:12)

You can be saved: John 16:33 I have said these things to you, that in me you may have peace. In the world, you will have tribulation. But take heart; I have overcome the world.

Note: Replace all the lies told to you with the promises of God.

You are free, you are loved, and you are whole.

EPILOGUE

I want you to read this vow to yourself in the mirror:

I promise to love you, despite your failures and imperfections. It is okay if you have failed. You can get back up. You deserve to be loved and deserve to have respected boundaries. Despite the words of others, your feelings are valid. Your experiences have made you a better version of yourself. I promise to be kind to you, especially in moments of brokenness.

ABOUT THE AUTHOR

Beatrice Belinda is a devoted Christian mother of two girls. She currently lives in Florida and is trying to change the world by inspiring hope and change. She was a photographer in her former career and a current psychology student. Here is to a new journey as an author! *The depths of his love* is her official first book.

You can find more from her at:

www.beatricebelinda.com